Foolish Ostrich
(A Bushman legend)

Written by
Cath Jones

Illustrated by
Ruth Waters

In the beginning, Mantis had fire.

But he kept it for himself.

He did not give it to the living things in the world, because he did not think they were ready for it.

Fire would just hurt them.

But Mantis knew that Ostrich was a clever and stubborn bird.

He knew that if he gave fire to Ostrich, she would keep it safe.

And if someone did take fire from clever Ostrich, then they would be worthy of having fire!

Mantis went down into the valley to visit Ostrich.

Clever Ostrich was happy to help.

She took fire and hid it under one of her wings. She knew it would be safe there.

Mantis told Ostrich to take good care of fire.

Then he left.

But soon the First Bushman saw the flickering flames.

He knew that fire was hidden under Ostrich's wing!

"If I had fire," he said to himself, "I could cook with it and have heat. I must steal it from her. I will flatter and trick Ostrich and get fire for myself!"

When Ostrich saw the First Bushman coming to see her, she kept fire well-hidden under her wing.

She knew that he would want it.

"Good morning, clever Ostrich," said the First Bushman. "I had a dream about you last night. In my dream, you could fly!"

"Fly?" said Ostrich. "How?"

"It was dawn and you were standing on top of a hill," said the First Bushman. "You had your wings open and your eyes shut!"

Ostrich could not resist the chance to fly.

So the next morning, at dawn, she set off for the top of a big hill.

She shut her eyes and spread out her wings.

But the First Bushman was waiting!

The First Bushman was well-hidden and Ostrich did not spot him!

He crept out and stole fire from under Ostrich's wing.

Then he ran off!

This was such a shock for Ostrich. She was so upset.

She still could not fly, but now she had lost fire as well!

From that day on, she was not Clever Ostrich.

She was Foolish Ostrich!

And from that day forth, Mankind had fire.